Elsa Schiaparelli

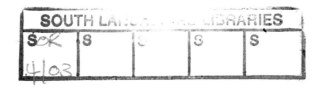
08853540

Translated from the French by Jane Brenton

First Published in Great Britain in 1997
by Thames and Hudson Ltd, London

British Library Cataloguing-in-Publication Data

A catalogue record for this book is available from
the British Library
ISBN 0-500-01784-0

Printed and bound in Italy

Elsa Schiaparelli

Text by François Baudot

Thames and Hudson

What remains today of the house of Schiaparelli, 21 Place Vendôme, Paris? The name still lingers, like the sting of a whiplash. That signature S, wafting its delicious perfume of scandal and success: Shocking! – like the pink that became synonymous with the colourful personality of Elsa Schiaparelli herself. As for the clothes, though the label ceased to exist when the designer retired in 1953, they have an enduring fascination for anyone interested in the history of fashion or the social history of the inter-war period because they epitomize fashion that is constantly being reinvented, constantly renewed. They provide proof that the most individual genius can be fulfilled in the practice of couture. Profoundly original, they nevertheless take account of functional constraints. It is this blend of individuality and discipline that has been seized on by modern designers. If two of the best – Yves Saint Laurent and Jean-Paul Gaultier – tend to work in a series of abrupt leaps from one season to the next, forging a style by way of a succession of dazzling masterstrokes, it is because of 'Schiap'; it is to her that they owe this abiding principle of subversion, of shocking in order to entertain, provoking in order to conquer. 'Beauty will be convulsive or it will not be beauty,' wrote André Breton in *Nadja*. That was very much the principle Schiaparelli always followed and indeed, in her own individual way, perfectly exemplified – though she would have been a bit more down to earth. In her autobiography, *Shocking Life*, she wrote: 'Two words have always been banned from my house – the word "création", which strikes me as the height of pretentiousness, and the word "impossible".' Nevertheless, with hindsight, we see her as the authentic artist that she most certainly was – one who, in the field of fashion, pushed back the frontiers of the possible.

We should remind ourselves that before Schiaparelli there was the egregious Paul Poiret and the ambitious Coco Chanel – two entirely different creative temperaments who represented even in those early years the two strands that were to run through the century, intertwined, contradictory but ultimately complementary. As the pendulum swung from one to the other, so the wardrobes of fashion-conscious women everywhere were filled with ever more various creations. In the space of barely ten years Elsa Schiaparelli, who had met Poiret and knew Chanel only too well from being so frequently compared with her, was to create the elaborate synthesis of classicism and outrageousness that still today represents the pinnacle of Parisian haute couture. It is appropriate to mention that the firm of Lesage, who even now produce embroidery for haute-couture collections, were Schiaparelli's closest associates during the thirties. Her original ideas reinvigorated the embroiderer's exquisite craft.

In her autobiography, Schiaparelli describes her first meeting with Poiret: 'It was then that I met Paul Poiret, whom I greatly admired and considered the greatest artist of his time. One day I accompanied a rich American friend to the small house bursting with colour which Paul Poiret had in the Rue St Honoré. It was my first visit to a *maison de couture*. While my friend was choosing lovely dresses, I gazed around moonstruck. Silently I tried things on and became so enthusiastic that I forgot where I was, and walked in front of the mirrors not too displeased with myself. I put on a coat of large, loose cut. . . . It was magnificent. "Why don't you buy it, *mademoiselle?* It might have been made for you." The great Poiret himself was looking at me. I felt the impact of our personalities.

"I cannot buy it," I said. "It is certainly too expensive, and when could I wear it?"

"Don't worry about money," said Poiret, "and *you* could wear anything anywhere."'

Literally captivated, Schiaparelli bore her gift back to the modest apartment she occupied at the time. Soon she would possess an entire wardrobe of clothes by the great Poiret.

but, revolutionary as it was, Poiret's version of glamour was very much confined to the enclosed world of the boudoir. The harem girl of the fashionable *quartiers*, the madonna of the divan, was not to throw off her shackles until the outbreak of the First World War. Then she would frequently be required to take the place of the men who had been sent to the front. More active, thinner, fitter, her hair cut short, her skirt hems raised, she stepped out into the real world. It was at that moment that Chanel chose to lay the foundations of the minimalist style which was to sweep all before it. And yet the tentative emergence in 1934 of the young Elsa Schiaparelli was enough to furrow Chanel's brow. Both designers occupied the same territory – moving frequently in the same circles – and they appeared to have identical cultural aspirations. Compared with these two, Madeleine Vionnet, the remaining member of the trio of formidable woman who dictated the 'look' and dominated between-the-wars chic, seemed traditional, hiding away discreetly behind the high quality of her workmanship.

After sack dresses, dropped waists and short boyish haircuts, 1928 brought a new emphasis on the female form. Unrestricted, tanned and fit, the body would henceforth dictate the shape of the garment rather than the garment the shape of the body. The breasts were gently moulded by the lacy cups of the brassiere, swelling out above a narrow torso liberated from its traditional corset. The waist occupied its natural position, the shoulders were narrow but exaggerated. Nothing more than a thin slip separated garment from skin. As for skirt lengths, during the day they stuck at mid-calf, but in the evening they plunged to the ground, in narrow fluid sheaths. There were busy touches at the neckline, a proliferation of jewels and frivolous accessories, embroidered motifs, and ornaments of one sort or another set against a plain background. And then, to complete the dashing silhouette (in a use of imagination in inverse proportion to size), the little hat that dotted the 'i' in Paris.

I n *Shocking Life*, Schiaparelli wrote, 'Once or twice I had thought that instead of painting or sculpture, both of which I did fairly well, I could invent dresses or costumes. Dress designing, incidentally, is to me not a profession but an art. I found that it was a most difficult and unsatisfying art, because as soon as a dress is born it has already become a thing of the past. As often as not too many elements are required to allow one to realize the actual vision one had in mind. The interpretation of a dress, the means of making it, and the surprising way in which some materials react – all these factors, no matter how good an interpreter you have, invariably reserve a slight if not bitter disappointment for you. In a way it is even worse if you are satisfied, because once you have created it the dress no longer belongs to you. A dress cannot just hang like a painting on the wall, or like a book remain intact and live a long and sheltered life.'

Despite this sobering thought, when she arrived in Paris, dresses were very much on Schiaparelli's mind. And yet there was nothing in her background to suggest a career in couture. The child of an eminent orientalist from Piedmont, she was born in 1890 and brought up in the Palazzo Corsini in Rome. She was also the niece of a famous astronomer, director of the observatory at Breda and the first person to establish the existence of canals on the planet Mars. This was a discovery of major significance, and Schiaparelli was frequently to cite her uncle as the reason why she was always 'moonstruck'. After a sheltered childhood, in the course of which she gave ample proof of the eccentricity that was always to be her hallmark, she met on a visit to England a lecturer who was half-Breton and half-Polish. Fascinated by his knowledge of theosophy, she married him and gave birth to a daughter, whom she named Gogo. When lack of money and marital disharmony led to divorce, she found herself a single mother but still young and free, and determined to make Paris her home. It was during this difficult period that she met Paul Poiret and became passionately interested in fashion.

One day, Schiaparelli was entertaining an American friend who was visiting Paris and she was struck by the rather unusual sweater her friend was wearing. Though simple, it was nonetheless extremely elegant. Discreet enquiries were made, and it turned out to have been knitted by an Armenian refugee, a woman who lived just round the corner from Schiaparelli. After Schiaparelli went to see her, the two became friends and decided to go into business together.

The new recruit agreed to use her needles to reproduce a simple design of a big white bow outstretched like a butterfly on a close-fitting black woollen top. To those of us today who are accustomed to the creations of Sonia Rykiel, this seems routine, and it is hard to imagine just how extraordinary it was at the time. Chanel had already made fashionable women accustomed to wearing knitted woollen dresses and jackets. But this time one was getting away from made-to-measure; this was in fact the beginning of what came to be known as sportswear. The American shop Strauss recognized its potential and immediately put in an order for forty sweaters, to be ready in a fortnight. In the attics of Paris, the Armenian community set to work and provided the launch-pad for Schiaparelli's glittering career. Schiaparelli was to remain good friends with her Armenian family, who later set up their own factory and became suppliers to the wholesale trade.

the house of Schiaparelli began life in three attic rooms on the Rue de la Paix. Over the doorway, beneath the name people found so difficult to pronounce, the couturier posted the prophetic sign 'Pour le Sport'. Then, with a combination of poetic imagination and sound common sense, this redoubtable young woman coolly set about making her mark on the world. From her earliest years she had been interested in artistic expression of all kinds, and she decorated her second series of sweaters with motifs inspired by Africa, then extremely fashionable through the work of the Cubists. Next came designs based on sailors' tattoos: snakes and anchors alternated with hearts pierced by arrows. After that came the skeleton jersey, the white lines on which echoed the design of the ribs, so that the female silhouette looked as if it were being viewed through an X-ray. Wriggling fishes began to appear on her bathing suits, lobsters on her fabrics. Trompe-l'oeil flies popped up on lengths of silk tulle. From Lindbergh, who had just flown the Atlantic, she borrowed the flying suit, which she adapted to suit her own model heroine – the woman who skied and swam and played golf by day and at night swayed to the syncopated beat of jazz or the tango. Schiaparelli's first evening ensemble of long dress with matching jacket comprised a simple sheath of black crêpe de Chine, and a white jacket with long sashes that crossed at the back. Reproduced the world over, this utterly plain outfit had a functional elegance that made it one of her greatest hits, allowing the house of Schiaparelli to achieve lift-off. A year later, in 1934, Schiaparelli moved to a corner of the Place Vendôme, just by the Ritz, the centre of sophisticated life and the haunt of pretty, wealthy young women eager to kick over the traces and rewrite the rules. With these women in mind, she devoted the ground floor of her new kingdom to a range of 'boutique' clothes. The shop was the first of its kind, though the idea was soon copied by most of the other big designers. It was Schiaparelli who came up with the winning formula of *prêt-à-porter*, which was destined to revolutionize fashion. The boutique stocked evening sweaters designed to be worn over long skirts, blouses and the readymade accessories scorned by the rest of haute couture.

From the mid-thirties onwards, Schiaparelli's collections were orchestrated around specific themes, and there was not one that did not cause a sensation. The first was called 'Stop, Look and Listen'. It included tweeds and raincoats as evening wear, embroidered saris, dresses made of glass and buttons made of French louis, mocking the notion of devaluation. 'Schiaparelli collection enough to cause crisis in vocabulary,' wrote one of the big newspapers. 'Schiap' was about to launch the zip fastener. Even her evening dresses suddenly bristled with zips in the most unlikely places. She had a fabric printed with newsprint, out of which the manufacturers did very well, selling thousands of yards. For the Americans, suffering straitened domestic circumstances during the Depression, she offered kitchen aprons that would not have been out of place worn by Marie-Antoinette at the Trianon. She understood that life would never be the same again, that it would be lived at a different pace and would look different. Women no longer had the time or the paid help to make frequent changes of clothes, yet they still wanted to be fashionable in a way that took account of the requirements of what people still referred to as 'modern life'. But where Elsa Schiaparelli really let herself go was in the details. There was a hat whose convolutions echoed those of the human brain, a pointed clown's hat, a lamb cutlet hat, a hat in the shape of a shoe, a telescopic hat, and so on. There was the grasshopper look, suits whose pockets were like drawers, novelty buttons shaped like lips or animals, feathers, paperweights, padlocks, sticks of barley sugar or glass eyes. . . . There were the first bracelets and earrings in clear plastic. . . . Schiaparelli's innovations were so many and so various that the list is endless. The collections leading up to the German invasion were called 'Musical Instruments', 'Butterflies', the 'Pagan Collection' (in which the women looked as if they had stepped out of a painting by Botticelli, with wreaths and delicate flower petals embroidered on flowing classical robes) and the 'Astrological Collection', with horoscopes, stars, moon and sun glittering with finely embroidered golden rays. The most exciting of all was the 'Circus' collection, inspired by Barnum. The elegant salons and staircases decorated by Jean-Michel Frank became the backdrop for Schiaparelli's parade of tightrope-walkers and jugglers, as well as Grock and the Fratellinis. Clowns, elephants and trapeze-artists appeared on the garments themselves which, on occasion, bore the words 'Attention à la peinture' – 'Wet Paint'. Handbags were shaped like balloons, gloves looked like white spats, and ice-cream cones perched on the models' heads. The fashion show spectaculars to which we are invited by Kenzo, Mugler and Galliano were invented right here.

●

It was characteristic of Elsa Schiaparelli to make generous acknowledgment of the contribution made by the talented artists she invited to work with her. As she wrote in her autobiography: 'Working with artists like Bébé Bérard, Jean Cocteau, Salvador Dali, Vertès, Van Dongen; and with photographers like Hoyningen-Huene,

Horst, Cecil Beaton and Man Ray gave one a sense of exhilaration. One felt supported and understood beyond the crude and boring reality of merely making a dress to sell.' Dali designed for his good friend a telephone handbag in black velvet, its round dial embroidered in gold. There were other surrealist touches, too. Jean Cocteau designed embroidered motifs interspersed with poetic symbols, used on evening dresses. Jean Hugo devised buttons that are also little sculptures – the hallmark of the Schiaparelli suit of the day. And Elsa Triolet and Louis Aragon created for Schiap a necklace made of aspirins. Imagination ran riot and the unexpected was the order of the day, to the point that in those anxious months before the Second World War, women from the most conventional backgrounds applauded these unlikely inventions.

The world of cinema also played its part in fostering Schiaparelli's talent, primarily because so many film stars loved to appear in her dazzling creations. Katharine Hepburn, for example, claimed that the studios thought she was too thin to be attractive and that her career only really took off when she began to frequent the salons at the Place Vendôme. Other regular callers included Claudette Colbert, Merle Oberon, Norma Shearer, and later Lauren Bacall on the arm of Humphrey Bogart. The shy Gary Cooper used to take all his conquests there. Then there were the Europeans: first Marlene Dietrich, then Annabella, Simone Simon, Michèle Morgan. One evening, Cécile Sorel wanted to see how the cape she had just had made would float behind her, so she ordered her chauffeur to drive her little open-topped sports car round and round the Place Vendôme, while she stood in the back. Arletty, famous for her elegance, wore Schiaparelli both on stage and off. 'Between 1930 and 1940, she turned fashion upside down. I still remember Schiap's glamour. She was the one who dressed me the best, according to my mood and how I happened to feel. She was an international star,' the actress would recall later, in conversation with her biographer Denis Demontion (*Arletty*, Flammarion). One such Schiaparelli design was a coat of many colours called Arlequin, a small masterpiece from the 'Commedia dell'Arte' collection.

But the film star whose image, through no desire of her own, will be for ever associated with Schiaparelli is Mae West. 'She was stretched out on the operating-table of my work-room, and measured and probed with care and curiosity. She had sent me all the most intimate details of her famous figure, and for greater accuracy a plaster statue of herself quite naked in the pose of the Venus de Milo.' Sadly, Miss West was never to return, not even to be fitted for her extraordinary costumes in *Every Day's a Holiday*, directed by Edward Sutherland in 1937. However, the rather suggestive life-size figure that languished in the workroom at Place Vendôme provided Léonor Fini with the inspiration for the design of the bottle for Schiaparelli's first perfume. This was, of course, the legendary 'Shocking'.

Subsequently, all the perfumes were given names starting with the letter S. As with Schiaparelli's haute couture, a lot of thought and imagination went into the concept associated with each perfume. Dali designed the bottle for 'Roi Soleil'. The design for the bottle for 'Sleeping', according to him, was based on a candle-holder, and the packaging was in the shape of a candle-extinguisher. The first perfume for men, 'Snuff', had a bottle shaped like a pipe. The series continued with 'Shut', 'Succès fou', 'Salut', etc., until war finally loomed, sounding the death knell for such frivolities.

●

In 1939, when the first panic had subsided, Schiaparelli asked her workforce to accept a cut in wages. Business was bad. Six hundred employees had dwindled to one hundred and fifty. As she related in *Shocking Life*, 'We built up a collection in three weeks, hoping for some response. This was the "cash and carry" collection with huge pockets everywhere so that a woman, obliged to leave home in a hurry or to go on duty without a bag, could pack all that was necessary to her. . . . There was an evening dress camouflaged to look like a day dress. When one emerged from the subway at night to attend a formal dinner, one merely pulled a ribbon and the day dress was lengthened into an evening dress. There was the Maginot Line blue, the Foreign Legion red, the aeroplane grey, the woollen boiler suit that one could fold on a chair next to one's bed so that one could put it on quickly in the event of an air-raid driving one down to the cellar.' Necessity was very much the mother of invention. . . . Schiap described how she printed on a scarf Maurice Chevalier's last refrain: 'Monday – no meat. Tuesday – no alcohol. Wednesday – no butter. Thursday – no fish. Friday – no meat. Saturday – no alcohol . . . but Sunday – *toujours l'amour.*'

Forced to flee the invasion forces, Schiaparelli sought refuge in the United States, where she had many friends. With the energy and imagination that never deserted her, she threw herself into relief work. Meanwhile, at the Place Vendôme, things were kept ticking over by the shop manager, Bettina Bergery – wife of the unpredictable Gaston Bergery, friend of Léon Blum, founder of the Parti Populaire Française and subsequently ambassador of the Vichy government. After the Liberation, Schiaparelli returned to take up the reins. But times had changed; Christian Dior's star was rising fast. The New Look swept away a modernist fantasy that endured scarcely longer than the spirit that engendered it. Schiaparelli, highly respected, surrounded by *objets d'art* and blessed with a circle of famous friends (musicians, writers, painters and journalists), determined to retire. From then on, she divided her time between the splendid house, now demolished, in the Rue de Berry, and Hammamet in Tunisia, which she helped to popularize. Her daughter Gogo married the diplomat Berri Berenson, a union which produced two daughters, Marisa and Berinthia. The former became a famous model and later an actress, exhibiting just that sense of elegance that her grandmother, the 'shocking' doyenne of fashion, never tired of questioning and reevaluating. Hers was an inventive spirit, in which powers of creativity were matched by a sense of beauty and a childlike simplicity of vision: ephemeral, and constantly reinvented.

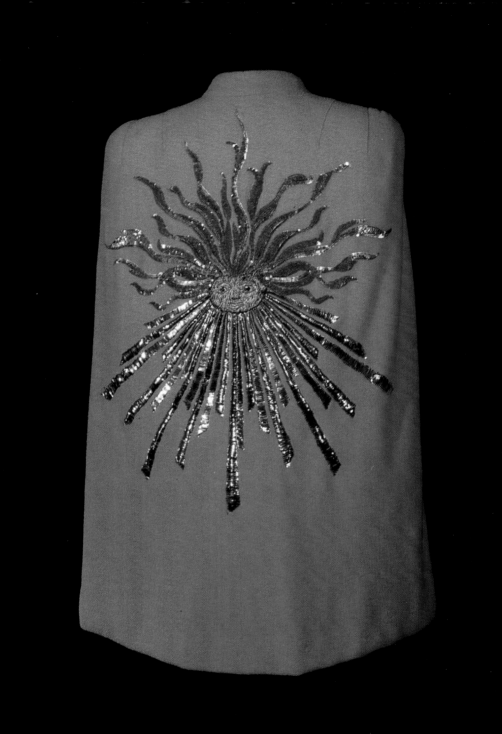

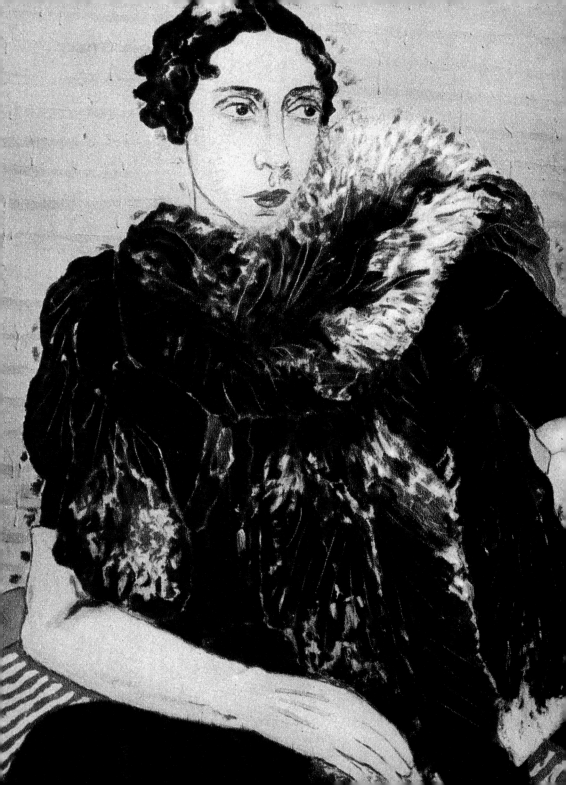

Schiaparelli's new silhouette —
rigid shoulders, neat waist,
brief skirt, surprising colours.
Wool jacket and skirt;
silk blouse. And a nose-diving
feathered hat.
Bonwit Teller

Bérard

Robe de Schiaparelli - 193X.

créé par Jean Cocteau.

Schiaparelli

A gray linen dress embroidered with Cocteau's design—hair golden, lips pink, eyes peacock blue and a blue Cellophane hand kerchief. Hattie Carnegie.

Chanel

White marocain twinkling with black paillettes, a black ribbon belt and a mad coiffure concocted of ribbon, feathers and a pailletted veil. Salon de Couture, Bonwit Teller.

VOGUE

including
CLOTHES FOR TH
NORTH AND SOU

JULY 20, 1938 (15)
ONE SHILLING

FOR CONDITIONS OF SALE OF SUPPLY SEE
THE CONDÉ NAST PUBLICATIONS LTD

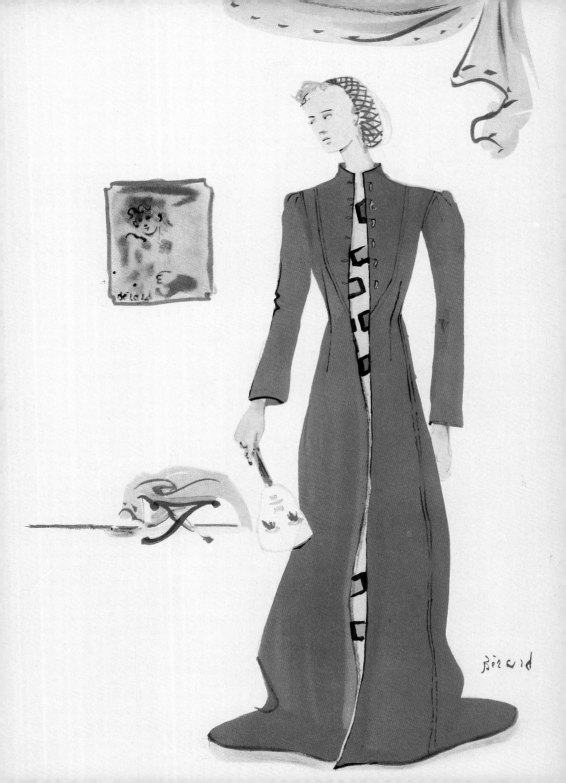

Bérard

Circus parade at Schiaparelli's

Shocking
de
Schiaparelli

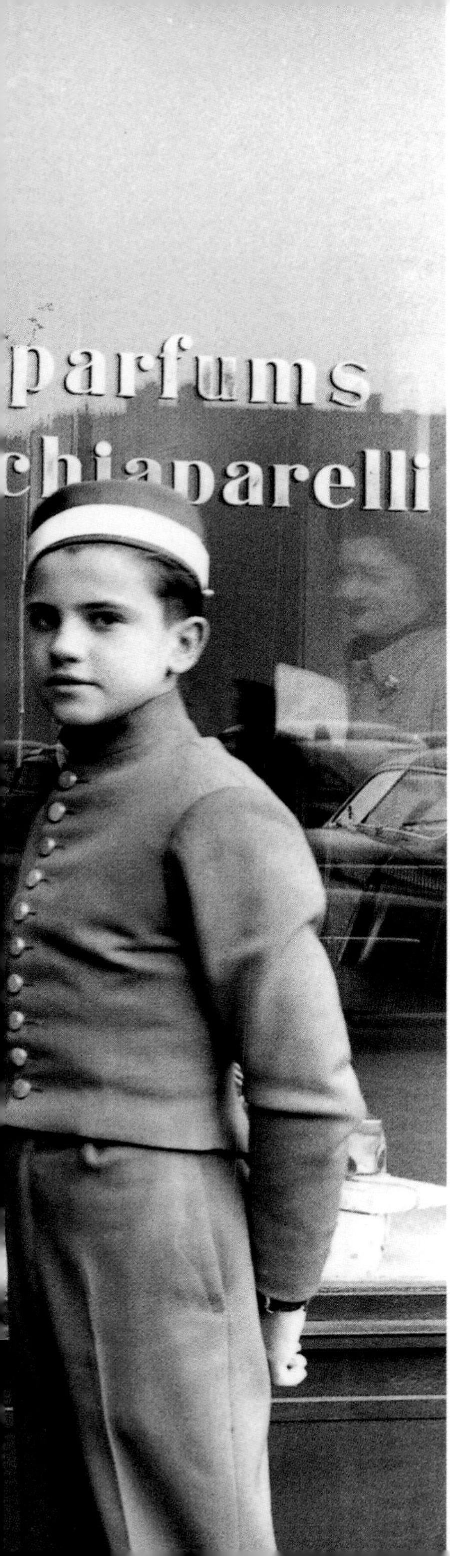
parfums
chiaparelli

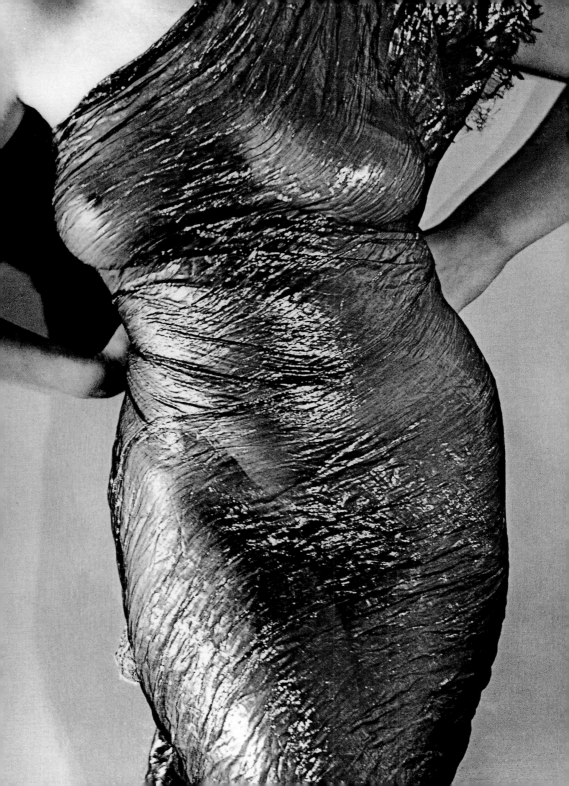

Schiaparelli a fait cette robe pour la danse. Je l'as copiée pour le Harper's Bazaar

Jean

1937

PARIS

Schiaparelli might have cut this tapering
sheath for Madame Tallien. A slit for the

Chronology

1890 Born on 10 September in Rome, where she spends her childhood.

1913 First trip to Paris and discovery of the rue de la Paix. Period spent in London. Meets William de Wendt.

1914 Marries William de Wendt. Outbreak of war.

1915 Leaves for Nice with her husband.

1919 With her husband, makes first journey to the United States, where she gets to know Marcel Duchamp and Picabia. Birth of her daughter, Yvonne.

1921 Following her divorce the previous year, Schiaparelli finds herself with little money. Starts to work with Gaby Picabia who imports French clothing until Gaby's departure for Paris. She then works as a translator for a firm of importers. Meets Alfred Stieglitz and Man Ray.

1922 Returns to Paris. Frequents Le Bœuf sur le Toit restaurant where she meets Picabia again, together with Tristan Tzara and the Dadaists. Opening of her first atelier on the rue de Seine, where she designs knitwear and sportswear. Meets Paul Poiret and begins to design dresses.

1927 Opening of a boutique at 4, rue de la Paix. Sweaters with butterfly bows and tie a success. Creation of first town outfits. Jean Clément begins to work for her as a designer of accessories.

1929 First full collection leads 'Schiap' to be described by the press as 'one of the rare creative talents' of the moment. Shortly afterwards, she starts to work with Roger Jean-Pierre.

1930 Creation of the Mad Cap bonnet, an immediate success. First evening ensemble.

1933 Travels to the United States to promote her designs. Dresses Katharine Hepburn. Opening of a boutique in London.

1934 Launch of three perfumes, *Salut*, *Souci* and *Schiap*, created in her perfume atelier at Bois-Colombe.

1935 Moves to 21, Place Vendôme, surrounded by the works of Giacometti and interiors designed by Jean-Michel Frank. The atelier is frequented by the Duchess of Windsor, Greta Garbo and Gloria Guinness. Arletty abandons Lanvin to become one of Schiaparelli's models.

Astonishing draped effect in this 1952 evening gown photographed
by Henry Clarke for American Vogue. One of Schiaparelli's last designs,
it shows her adapting to the innovations of the 'New Look'.
Photo: Henry Clarke. © ADAGP, Paris 1996.

1936	'Parachute' collection and dress.
1937	'Music' collection. Success of the shoe-shaped hat which becomes the emblem of the imaginative accessories created by Schiaparelli. These included telescopic hats and buttons in the shape of crayfish, lobsters or swans.
1938	Launch of the perfumes *Sleeping* and *Shocking*, the latter in the celebrated bust-shaped bottle (that of Mae West . . .). 'Circus' collection with embroidery executed by the Lesage ateliers. Phoebus and Char d'Apollon capes.
1939	Creation of *Snuff*, the first perfume for men. 'Cash and Carry' collection. Leaves for the United States, where she remains until 1945. Comtesse Haydn manages the fashion house in her absence.
1940	Signs her first licence agreement with Kaiser, a stocking manufacturer.
1945	Returns to France, where she takes up the reins of her fashion house again. Her collections continue to enjoy extraordinary success in post-war America. Pierre Cardin and Hubert de Givenchy work for a while in her ateliers.
1946–1947	Launch of the 'Roi Soleil' perfume, with a bottle designed by Salvador Dali. Creation of a luggage collection suited to the new lifestyle of women after the war and of the travel coats with 'suitcase' pockets which were judged prophetic by American *Vogue*.
1949	Her new collection makes the cover of *Newsweek*. Opening of a branch to oversee the distribution of the prêt-à-porter collection in the United States, while sales were restricted to one boutique per city in order to maintain a certain 'exclusiveness'.
1952	Robin Hood hat and variation of the Mad Cap. 'Shocking Elegance' collection. The financial difficulties experienced by the Parisian fashion house since the end of the war continue to increase.
1954	Elsa Schiaparelli closes her fashion house and writes her memoirs. Right to the end of her life, she was to show a particular interest in Yves Saint Laurent and, above all, Balenciaga.
1973	Dies in her sleep at the age of 83.

The camouflage outfit of 1939 is symbolic of the witty and iconoclastic way in which Schiaparelli could observe objects and events. © Bernard Richebé.

Schiaparelli

The model Bettina portrayed by Henry Clarke in the *Figaro* album in 1949. Evening cape by Schiaparelli. Photo: Henry Clarke. © ADAGP, Paris 1996. Schiaparelli's imagination reached its peak in the accessories with which she embellished her outfits. These **gloves with long nails** were the perfect accompaniment to the Revolutionary coat. © Photo: Chantal Fribourg.

Pink silk cape embroidered with a golden sun. Part of the 'Astrological Collection' of 1938 for which Christian Bérard sketched three silhouettes. © Photo: Chantal Fribourg. Sketch: Christian Bérard. © All rights reserved.

Embroidered summer jacket designed in 1938 with buttons in the shape of circus horses. © Courtesy of the Board of Trustees of the Victoria and Albert Museum.
Long black woollen coat with six pink velvet pockets in the shape of *jardinières*, each embroidered with gold thread, tiny white porcelain roses and purple sequins by François Lesage. Winter 1938–39. Materials combined in this way are often found in Schiap's work. © Coll. UFAC.

Two aspects of Elsa Schiaparelli: on the left, seen by the painter Laglenne in 1932; © Coll. Kharbine-Tapabor; and photographed by Man Ray in 1934; © Man Ray Trust/ADAGP, Paris 1997. In the latter she wears a feather cape over a pleated silk gown.

Theatrical setting for this androgynous Robin Hood, whose stark outfit bears witness to the designer's wish to reduce the differences between the male and female silhouette. © Photo: Cecil Beaton. Courtesy of Sotheby's, London.

Tight waist, straight shoulders and large patch pockets are characteristic of Schiaparelli's designs, while the woollen fabrics were dyed in colours or with patterns invented by the couturière. © Philadelphia Museum of Art. Illustration by Christian Bérard. Courtesy *Vogue*. © 1935 (renewed 1963, 1991) by The Condé Nast Publications, Inc.

This evening dress, from the Summer 1937 collection, in black crêpe printed with large white butterflies perfectly embodies the spirit behind Schiaparelli's designs. Her earliest creations were knitted sweaters which already incorporated all sorts of motifs: bows, butterflies or Cubist designs. These sweaters marked the beginning of her success. © Coll. UFAC.

Drawing by Jean Cocteau. Dessin Cocteau. © All rights reserved.
Linen cross-over jacket, decorated with a bold embroidered motif, reproducing a design specially created for Schiaparelli by Jean Cocteau in 1937. Philadelphia Museum of Art, gift of Elsa Schiaparelli.

In Schiaparelli's work, the garment is often simply a pretext for displaying embroidery to advantage, as in the case of this 1937 evening cape executed by François Lesage from a drawing by Jean Cocteau. Philadelphia Museum of Art, gift of Elsa Schiaparelli. © Photo: Patrice Stable.
Embroidered motif in gold thread in the shape of a padlock executed by François Lesage. © All rights reserved.

The photographer Horst began a lengthy collaboration with the Condé Nast group in the 1930s. In almost fifty years of picture taking, he would establish lasting friendships with the principal celebrities of his time.
© Photo: Horst P. Horst.
A Schiaparelli model wearing the Sentinelle cape, November 1936.
© Roger-Viollet.

Sumptuous jacket in black velvet designed in 1939, with two embroidered gold and silver motifs in the shape of Baroque mirrors. © The Metropolitan Museum of Art, gift of Mrs Pauline Potter, 1950.
Evening ensemble (1937) and evening jacket (1938). These designs typify Schiaparelli's work and are admirable for the attention paid to detail: cut-out or embroidered pockets, collar openings, the originality of the buttons. © The Metropolitan Museum of Art, gift of Mrs Keagy, 1974 and Julia Henry, 1978.

The various sketches for hats produced in 1937 for the House of Schiaparelli include the shoe-hat, suggested to Salvador Dali by his wife Gala. © Coll. UFAC.
Outfit for early evening wear in green silk velvet, embroidered with gold flowers in relief. © Coll. Kharbine-Tapabor.

A collector of *objets d'art* of all periods, Elsa Schiaparelli received the whole of Paris in her home on the rue de Berry. © Photo: Jean-Pierre Sudre. Private collection of Marquise Cacciapuoti.
Elsa Schiaparelli. © Photo: Piaz. Private collection of Marquise Cacciapuoti.

Quilted red Pekinese cape (1933) worn over a grey satin sheath dress. Elsa Schiaparelli caused a sensation when she wore it to a concert at the Théâtre des Champs-Elysées. © Horst P. Horst.
Illustration of a quilted beach-robe for the cover of American *Vogue*, July 1938. © All rights reserved.

Insect necklace. Seen from a distance, the transparency of the necklace's support gave the impression that real insects were crawling round the wearer's neck. © Brooklyn Museum, gift of Paul and Arturo Peralta-Ramos.
Elsa Schiaparelli and Salvador Dali maintained a fruitful friendship long after their collaboration was over. Dali at Neuilly in 1949. © Archives Snark.

Salvador Dali, *Lobster Telephone,* 1937. © Demart Pro Arte B. V., Geneva/ADAGP, Paris 1997.
The same year (1937), Schiaparelli drew inspiration from the lobster for an evening gown in painted silk muslin. Former collection of the Duchess of Windsor. © Philadelphia Museum of Art, gift of Elsa Schiaparelli.

Revolutionary coat with masculine cut: wide shoulders and narrow hips. Illustration by Christian Bérard. Courtesy *Vogue.* © 1935 (renewed 1963, 1991) by The Condé Nast Publications, Inc. Schiaparelli widely promoted the Surrealist aesthetic in fashion, especially the purity of line which she appreciated above all else. Photo: André Durst. Courtesy *Vogue.*
© 1936 (renewed 1964, 1992) by The Condé Nast Publications, Inc.

Two pages of illustrations produced by her friend the painter Christian Bérard for *Vogue* in 1938, based on the designs Schiaparelli created for her 'Circus' collection. Illustration by Christian Bérard. Courtesy *Vogue.* © 1938 (renewed 1966, 1994) by The Condé Nast Publications, Inc.

Inspired by a bust of Mae West, the bottle for *Shocking,* the first perfume created by Schiaparelli. © Collection Kharbine-Topabor, 1945.
Four metallic buttons in the form of acrobats fasten this silk jacket created for the 'Circus' collection in 1938. Schiaparelli was renowned for the sculpture-buttons which characterized many of her suits. © Courtesy of the Board of Trustees of the Victoria and Albert Museum.

Schiaparelli addressing the crowd gathered in the stadium at Saint Paul, Minnesota, at the end of a lecture tour of the United States, November 1940. © All rights reserved.

A navy-blue woollen suit designed in 1938 demonstrates her eccentricity even in sobriety. Schiaparelli owned one of the best tailoring ateliers in Paris. In this suit, two breast pockets hug the entire length of the torso. © The Metropolitan Museum of Art, gift of J.R. Keagy, 1974.
Drawing illustrating **the Schiap look** in 1945. © Collection Kharbine-Topabor.

Embroidery sample made for Schiaparelli by François Lesage and featuring bunches of grapes. © Photo: Patrice Stable.
The classic bow-sash 'tailored' to suit Schiaparelli's iconoclastic couture and introducing the emblematic shocking pink. © Photo: Horst P. Horst.

During the thirties, **Marlene Dietrich** was one of Schiaparelli's most ardent followers, 1934. Photo: Walling Jr. © The Kobal Collection.
A typically Schiap invention: in preparation for the cold, a collar cut from one piece of material, matched to the jacket of this 1949 black grosgrain silk suit, comes right up to the nose, forming two points at the nape of the neck which can be brought back and knotted under the chin. © Photo: Horst P. Horst.

Christmas window display for Schiaparelli perfumes in 1952. © Photo: Edouard Boubat/Top.

Place Vendôme and the entrance to the Schiaparelli perfume shop. Fake birds and bottles of *Shocking* happily share a huge birdcage. © Photo: Man Ray Trust/ADAGP, Paris 1997.
The Torso was one of Schiaparelli's final creations. © Man Ray Trust/ADAGP, Paris 1997.

A Jean Cocteau illustration, after a Schiaparelli design, for the American magazine *Harper's Bazaar* in 1937. Drawing: Cocteau. © All rights reserved.
Splendour both in colour and in fabric, the legacy of the influence of Paul Poiret is seen in this fuchsia satin fingerless glove. © All rights reserved.

Two tricorn hats for Elsa Schiaparelli's 'crazy carnival' in 1938 captured by Erwin Blumenfeld. Photo: Erwin Blumenfeld. Courtesy *Vogue*. © 1938 by The Condé Nast Publications, Inc.
Portrait of Elsa Schiaparelli. Photo: Irving Penn. Courtesy *Vogue*. © 1948 by The Condé Nast Publications, Inc.

Bettina in a woollen coat photographed by Irving Penn. Courtesy *Vogue*. © 1950 (renewed 1978) by The Condé Nast Publications, Inc.
Surrealist setting for a coat with numerous pockets, both real or false. © Photo: Cecil Beaton. Courtesy of Sotheby's, London.

Chronology and captions translated by Ruth Taylor

The publishers wish to thank the House of Schiaparelli.

They would also like to thank the Marquise Cacciapuoti, Marisa Berenson, Mlle Laurence Benaïm and M. François Lesage.

Thanks are due also to: Edouard Boubat, Irving Penn, Horst P. Horst, Patrice Stable, Chantal Fribourg.

Finally, this book could not have been produced without the invaluable assistance of Nicole Chamson (ADAGP), Haydn Hansell (Victoria and Albert Museum), Olivier Saillard (Musée de la Mode de Marseille), Marie-Hélène Poix (Musée de la Mode et du Textile), Philippe (Kharbine-Tapabor), Tiggy Maconochie (Hamilton Photographers), Michèle (Vogue), Frank Munoz (Telimage), Pierre Pigaglio (AFDPP), Lorraine Mead (The Condé Nast Publications, Inc.), Sylvianne (Scoop), Lydia Cresswell-Jones (Sotheby's, London) and Christine Lloyd Lyons (The Kobal Collection).

Our thanks to them all.